WORLD-BUILDING GAMES

What does it take to build something as iconic as the Empire State Building, or as awe-inspiring as a rocket that flies into space? What's the secret to putting together a bustling, thriving farm or some of the greatest platforming levels ever seen? It takes hard work, dedication, and a bit of luck. Or, perhaps, it just takes the right game!

Everyone knows the world-building joy that comes from putting together towering, sprawling structures in *Minecraft*, but there are so many other games out there, offering similar thrills. *Terraria*, *Stardew Valley*, and *LEGO Worlds* are some of the biggest world-building games around, and we've got inside access to the games that let you unleash your wild creativity in ways that will startle and amaze your friends. Also, if you're a *Minecraft* fan, we've got secrets that not even a veteran will know, plus amazing tips to help you become a *Minecraft* master!

CONTENTS

FEATURES

50

THE BIGGEST GAMES

44

26

40

CONTENTS

34

30

20

EDITOR IN CHIEF
Jon White, Ryan King

EDITOR
Stephen Ashby

CONTRIBUTORS
Adam Barnes, Ross Hamilton, Oliver Hill, Simon Miller,
Dom Peppiatt, Dominic Reseigh-Lincoln, Ed Smith,
Paul Walker-Emig, Josh West

LEAD DESIGNER
Greg Whitaker

DESIGNER
Anne-Claire Pickard

PRODUCTION
Sanne de Boer, Hannah Westlake, Carrie Mok, Jen Neal

COVER IMAGES

ISBN 978-1-338-11047-0
10 9 8 7 6 5 4 3 2 1   16 17 18 19 20
Printed in the U.S.A.   40
First printing, September 2016

29 MINECRAFT SECRETS

EVERYTHING YOU NEED TO KNOW!

Considering how long the game has been out and how many people play it, you'd think there isn't much more to learn about *Minecraft* at this point. Well, there are many secrets to the block-building game that not everyone knows. Why enemies act like they do, for example, or how you can use torches to breathe underwater. There are a lot of ways the world of *Minecraft* works, and you'll need to know them!

We've tracked down the biggest and the best secrets hidden within the game. Some will help you play the game better; others are just cool little facts. Read along and see how many you already know!

UNLIMITED WATER

01 Water is an essential resource. Perhaps you'd like a pool in the back of your mansion. It has more useful features, too, letting you create cool underwater bases or using it to water your crops in the field.

However, trekking all the way to the nearest water source can be a pain, which is why this handy little trick is so great. Simply dig out four blocks in a square and use two buckets of water on opposite corners to fill it. Now, when you fill a bucket from the pool, it will automatically refill. Unlimited water!

ENDERMEN PROTECTION

02 These guys are a nuisance, but there's an easy solution. Pick up a pumpkin and place it on your head. It'll be hard to see, but you'll stare Endermen in the eyes without concern.

HIDDEN COMPASS

03 Without a map or compass? Look down at the ground and start to dig; you'll notice the cracks as you bash the block point in a certain direction. They head north to help you orientate!

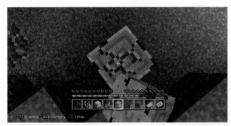

BREATHE UNDERWATER

04 This is handy for those who like to explore underwater. Take a stack of torches and place them on a nearby rock for a temporary block of fresh air. Just ensure your head is in the same block as the torch before you place it.

29 MINECRAFT SECRETS

LET TORCHES DO THE WORK

05 Don't manually dig up all that pesky sand or gravel ... offload the work to something else—like the handy torch! Place a torch under a block of sand/gravel. As each block falls, it turns into an item you can pick up.

FESTIVE CHEER!

06 Play *Minecraft* at Christmastime and you'll find a very merry Easter egg. Every chest in the game, either small or large, will have their skins replaced with Christmas presents to make finding these in a dungeon more rewarding.

USE HALF SLABS

07 Did you know that half slabs of wood are fire-resistant? It takes more effort to craft using half-slabs, but if you take the time to build with these it'll never set aflame. All half-slabs are stronger than normal blocks, too!

HEROBRINE

08 Legend has it that in the early days of *Minecraft* one player was visited by a character that would become known as Herobrine. This character, who looked exactly like your default character, Steve, except for bright-white eyes, appeared very briefly, said nothing, then disappeared. No one has seen Herobrine since, but the developer Mojang has regularly referenced the oddity in its patch notes by adding "Removed Herobrine" from the list of changes. Whether Herobrine was real or just a fantasy created by a very imaginative *Minecraft* player somewhere, we may never know ...

HOW TO HIDE!

09 Are you playing online and want to hide from friends? If you crouch, your name disappears from the screen. So if you want to hide in their house you can get the jump on them!

STOPPING WATER AND LAVA

10 Frustrated by flowing water and lava getting in your way? By placing blocks that don't completely fill a whole cube—like signs and pressure plates—you can block the flow of liquids!

QUICKER WATER

11 Some players use flowing water to create easy item transportation systems. You can increase the speed of flowing water by having it run across ice. It's tricky to craft such blocks, but it's a quicker transport method.

MINCERAFT

12 This hidden secret is very unlikely to appear for you, and you may not notice it! On the menu screen of the game, you'll see the *Minecraft* logo at the top. There's a very small chance that each time you see this screen it will actually load with the title "*Minceraft*".

MULTICOLORED SHEEP

13 In the PC version of *Minecraft* you can name certain creatures yourself, and some names have very unique secrets attached to them. Naming a sheep "jeb_" (with the underscore) will make that sheep's wool cycle through all the colors!

THE FAR LANDS

14 It sounds so mystical: a place at the end of the world where everything is glitched. The Far Lands was a place at the limit of *Minecraft's* randomized world generation, where the game could not properly control everything that happens. There were large structures of rocks with unusual shapes, and many interactions were bugged. This area of the map would appear at roughly 12

million blocks from your starting point, so it took a long walk to get there.

When the 1.8 patch was released, sadly the Far Lands was removed, and various barriers put in place to stop players from going that far. It's sort of a secret history of *Minecraft*, and early players would spend hours searching for these strange lands.

DOUBLE THE DANGER!

15 In rare cases, a spider will spawn with a skeleton riding on its back, known as a Spider Jockey. The skeleton and spider each have their own health, so you have to take them both down.

STAMPY ISLAND

16 Play on the console version of *Minecraft* to find this hidden secret to the northeast: an old version of the house YouTuber Stampylonghead built in his videos, and his boat, the S.S. *Stampy*.

NATURE'S BRIDGE

17 Do you like having a more natural bridge leading to your castle in the water? Well, if you collect lily pads from the swamp areas you can place them on top of water. Then you can use them as a sturdy footpath.

HALLOWEEN MONSTERS

18 Play *Minecraft* on October 31—Halloween—to see a twist to the monsters. Skeletons will appear with pumpkins on their heads, and while it doesn't change much, it's certainly fun.

TALKING ENCHANTMENTS

19 Ever wonder what the symbols on the enchantment table mean? It's actually the exact same alphabet used in an old game called *Commander Keen*. Some of the translations even have hidden meanings, like *"Elder Scrolls."*

COLLECTING MUSIC DISCS

20 You've probably found a music disc while exploring the dungeons, and there are only two to find hidden here. There are 12 in total, and they can be found by having a skeleton kill a creeper with its bow and arrows.

This is a pretty tricky thing to do, since a skeleton will generally stay away, while a creeper tries to get closer to you. The trick is to use various blocks as a trap that will keep the creeper in place while you position yourself so the skeleton hits the creeper, not you. It takes practice, but have patience.

Now playing: C418 - chirp

Creative △ Inventory Eject Mine

29 MINECRAFT SECRETS

UPSIDE-DOWN CREATURES

21 Next time you name an animal, try "Dinnerbone" or "Grumm." These are the nicknames of developers at Mojang, and any creature named this will turn upside down! They'll still move and act normally, except their feet will flail in the air!

HOW THE CREEPER WAS MADE

22 Did you know that when creating the monsters and animals for the game, the developer accidentally altered the axis of the pig model that is used in the game, causing the animal to stand upright instead of walking on four legs. This was the inspiration for the creeper model that was used afterward.

WATERING THE FIELD

24 Have a field of grass you want to clear away, but can't be bothered to manually bash those weeds? Place a block of water on top. Wherever the water spreads will destroy the grass.

DEADMAU5'S EARS

23 The artist deadmau5 is a huge fan of the game. He's even featured in it! Change your name to "deadmau5" and you'll equip his trademark mouse ears!

A UNIQUE RABBIT

25 If you name a rabbit "Toast" it changes its skin to a black-and-white rabbit. This is the same skin as a player's rabbit named Toast, who sadly ran away. The developers were told about this, and included it as a cute secret.

GAME REFERENCES!

26 Many paintings you can place are references to other games. Many are retro classics, such as Nintendo's game *Donkey Kong*!

GRIM FANDANGO

27 The painting of a skeleton is not a reference to the enemies, but a game called *Grim Fandango*, made by LucasArts.

INTERNATIONAL KARATE

29 There are two paintings in the game that pay homage to this 1980s fighting game, one referencing the original *International Karate*, one showing its two-player equivalent.

KING'S QUEST

28 This painting refers to an old point-and-click game, *King's Quest*. This character also appears in another painting for *Space Quest*.

TIPS & TRICKS
MINECRAFT

6 ESSENTIAL TIPS

MINE DIAMONDS AND CRAFT ARMOR

01 Armor is vital to survival; crafting diamond armor should be your first priority, and requires you to mine with an iron pickaxe.

DEAL WITH MOBS

02 Mobs can kill you quickly. You can gain the upper hand by spreading out enemies. Try to get some distance between you and the mobs, and then use a ranged weapon to take them out one by one.

QUICK TRICKS

ENCHANT YOUR STUFF
Build an enchanting table and use it to upgrade your weapons with new abilities.

STOP WATER FLOW
To quickly prevent water access, place a ladder on one side of the leak.

GROW CROPS FASTER

03 Crops can provide you with food, but can be slow to fully produce if you don't select the correct type of ground. The quickest way to grow crops for harvest is to plant them on water-based farmland and make sure that you spread out your crops evenly.

CUSTOMIZE FURNITURE

04 Did you know you could customize your furniture? Simply select the furniture in question and open up your inventory where you'll find options to make subtle changes to the look of it.

TRADE BOOKS

05 Enchantment books are hard to come by, but are great for getting your hands on advanced armor and weapons. If you're in desperate need for one, try trading with local villagers, since on rare occasions, they'll have one available for lots of emeralds.

TAME HORSES

06 Horses are the best way to move across your world quickly. Taming them can take a lot of patience, however. Feed a wild horse enchanted apples or carrots to lower its temper and gain its trust.

EASILY DEFEAT BLAZE
Blazes are tough but throw a couple of snowballs at one to cool him off a little.

TAME THE WILDLIFE
Feed bones to wild wolves and they will soon become tamed and fight by your side!

MINECRAFT

MINECRAFT POCKET EDITION TIPS

Manage your hunger
Keep plenty of food in your inventory if you're mining for a long time. You can check hunger levels in the top right.

Use light sources
Torches are great for dark caves, but there are alternatives. Lava can be just as useful.

Improve your armor
The armor icons located to the top left indicate how much life is left in your current suit.

Quick switch
Don't go opening up your full inventory menu to switch between items—just tap them on-screen.

3 THINGS TO TRY

1 CREATE FIREWORKS
For a spectacular show, build your own rockets. The most basic rockets can be formed by combining paper and gunpowder.

2 BUILD GIANT STRUCTURES
Before starting in Creative Mode, make sure you have the correct blocks in your inventory, as well as an empty patch of ground to build on.

3 QUEST WITH FRIENDS
If you're playing on a harder difficulty level, consider joining friends and questing together. It may help you get through tough mines.

MASTER THE NETHER
CONQUER FORTRESSES AND COLLECT COOL LOOT

1 MAKE A NETHER PORTAL
Before entering the Nether, you need to create a portal. You'll need ten obsidian blocks, and flint and steel to activate it.

2 PROTECT YOUR PORTAL
Once in a while, you need to protect your portal. Watch out for Ghasts shooting fireballs and build a wall for your portal!

3 EXPLORE FORTRESSES
Nether fortresses are filled with goodies, including rarities. Go through any fortress and open chests as you go!

4 DEAL WITH THE WITHER
Wither skeletons are really dangerous and can infect you with the Wither if they touch you. Kill them before they get you!

5 HARVEST MAGMA CREAM
Kill all magma cubes that you come across—they can drop the brewing ingredient for a Fire Resistance Potion.

6 FIND A BLAZE SPAWNER
Look for floating Blazes and kill them until you get a Blaze rod for a Brewing Stand, then quickly escape!

BIGGEST GAMES OF 2017

This may have been a great year for games, but 2017 is already looking all killer, no filler! There's plenty to get excited about on the horizon, and in every kind of genre, too. From action-adventure to games that will drag you outdoors and have you rustling through long grass, 2017 is set to be one of the most exciting years for gaming. Don't get left out of the discussions, get up-to-date on the coolest games now and get hyped.

THE LEGEND OF ZELDA WII U

A new *The Legend Of Zelda* game is always cause for celebration, but 2017 is going to be super special. Link will go on his biggest adventure yet, exploring a gigantic open-world Hyrule with his trusty steed, Epona, and battling ancient evils. But it's the version on Nintendo's awesome upcoming NX system that has us truly excited. The more powerful console will make it look (somehow) even more beautiful.

BEYOND GOOD & EVIL 2

After years of delays, *Beyond Good & Evil 2* is finally on the way. The original 2003 action-adventure game was well received, putting journalist Jade on an epic adventure through cartoon conspiracies. The sequel is finally coming in 2017; so look forward to beautiful environments and fun action gameplay.

LEGO WORLDS

After a long time in beta, *LEGO Worlds* is close to release—a sprawling sandbox game that helps you build the truly crazy. It's a favorite of ours, thanks to its charming style and massive tool set; we imagine this actually has a chance of giving *Minecraft* a run for its money!

POKÉMON GO

For 20 years now, *Pokémon* games have challenged trainers to go out and catch 'em all. And now, with *Pokémon GO*, you can go out and do it in real life! This free-to-play augmented reality game communicates with your smartphone, beaming Pokémon out into the world for you to capture, train, and battle.

TERRARIA: OTHERWORLD

We love *Terraria*, and that's why we're so excited about *Terraria: Otherworld*! It isn't a direct sequel; instead it's a crazy "what if?" scenario taking us into a darker, sci-fi inspired world. *Otherworld* will feature a tighter, story-driven focus.

GAMES YOU'LL STILL BE PLAYING

We're in a golden era of gaming now; games don't live and die by the year they are released anymore. Some of the most awesome things happening in gaming in 2017 aren't new games, but the updates to your old favorites. Developers are now able to easily update your games with new content and features, meaning you don't have to pick up the latest titles to have a great time, and you can spend more time with games you love.

STARDEW VALLEY

Stardew Valley has blown us away. It's a surprise success story that delights with its charming farm-life gameplay and pixel-art graphics. And the game is only getting better. Despite being developed by one person, *Stardew Valley* is getting frequent updates, fixing bugs and generally ensuring that the game is as good as possible.

GUITAR HERO LIVE

The great thing about *Guitar Hero Live* is that it can be played forever because it's designed to be constantly updated with new music. It doesn't matter whether you're just getting into rock music or favor the softer sounds of pop, there's something for everyone on *Guitar Hero's* growing track list.

BESIEGE

This brilliant physics-based builder, where you construct medieval siege weapons to take out fortresses, isn't going to get old any time soon. The game was released as an Early Access title, which means the developer hadn't actually finished making the game, even though we were able to play it! That means we can expect lots of new tools to play with, and challenges to complete in future updates.

MINECRAFT

Microsoft and Mojang have big plans for *Minecraft* in 2017. Not only will they be adding new character skins and items, a HoloLens version is on the horizon that pulls *Minecraft* from your TV screen and out into the world around you. Search HoloLens on YouTube to check it out!

LEGO DIMENSIONS

LEGO Dimensions combines three of our favorite things: toys-to-life games, world-building, and, LEGO! Expect to see new DC and NINJAGO sets, as well as an array of heroes from *The LEGO Movie 2* and 2017's *LEGO Batman Movie*.

STATS

over **75** foes to conquer and banish from the world

200 crafting recipes for weapons, armor and potions

25 brick types to build whatever you want

13 million copies of *Terraria* have been sold globally

TERRARIA

GRAB YOUR TOOLS AND GO!

Being given the freedom to build your own worlds is seriously cool, and *Terraria* takes that to the limit with tons of blocks to choose from, tools to craft, and foes to face. With so much on offer, you'll need to use your imagination to craft your own world and decide what you want to build. But there are also various foes looking to kill you and a host of bosses that require plenty of skill to beat. Once you've started building, different *Terraria* characters will move into your creations and go about their daily lives. Keep all of these characters happy and they'll sell you items, weapons, and new blocks to help you on your epic journey. Progress further in the game and the enemies that you'll face will be even tougher. Are you up to the challenge? It's time to find out ...

TIPS & TRICKS

GRAPPLE EVERYWHERE
Use the grappling hook to move around the world fast and to jump over mobs.

SAVE YOUR ITEMS
The piggy bank is a great tool to have to double your inventory.

TOP 4 USER-CREATED BUILDINGS

MARKET

2 If you really want to take your *Terraria* journey to the next level, then building a market is a must. It's a great way of buying equipment and blocks to help you tackle foes and build better things.

WINDMILL

1 A lot of effort has gone into the building of this windmill. A motor block in the center powers the propellers, creating the look of it gliding through the air.

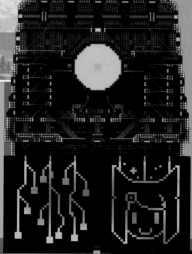

RAY GUN

4 We'd have preferred to shoot this ray gun, but it certainly looks the part. This building in particular was created by a group of users. You can tell it must have taken them a while just by looking at it.

TOWN

3 If you build a whole town, you'll soon find that characters fill up houses and shops. Ensure the buildings are connected so they can interact with one another.

EXCITE-O-METER

The latest update of *Terraria* is packed with cool stuff!

+ Extra bosses to fight
+ New areas to see
− Expert mode is super-tough!

LEAVE A TRAIL
When exploring a cave, leave campfires to help you find your way out.

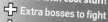

TERRARIA

TIPS & TRICKS

TERRARIA

6 ESSENTIAL TIPS

TO THE EDGE

01 The first thing you should do when starting up a new game is explore the edges of your new world. On either end of the map is a beach—follow it into the ocean and you'll find plenty of chests to get you started.

REVERSE GRAVITY

02 Gravitation Potions are common and can be useful for locating floating islands. Reversing gravity makes tracking down levitating strongholds easy, rewarding you with tasty loot early in the game.

QUICK TRICKS

KEEP A LIGHT
Stock yourself up with torches before going underground.

BLOOD MOON
This random event brings powerful monsters with it.

LINKED STORAGE

03 It might not be obvious but the piggy banks in *Terraria* are actually linked. Store something in a bank in one location and you can retrieve it from one in another. And the same goes for safes! If you're building away from your base then this can be a huge time-saver.

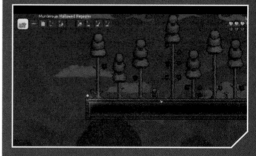

KNOW THE TIME

04 In-game time is important in *Terraria*. It impacts enemies that spawn, the effects of some items, and can make things harder to see. You can check the time on any in-game clock. Nighttime is from 7.30 P.M. to 4.30 A.M.

SAVE YOUR CASH

05 At some point, you're going to die in *Terraria*—it's unavoidable. If you know that you've got a few seconds to live and you don't want to forfeit the money you've collected, you can avoid losing it by moving the coins to your trash. Just don't forget they're there!

MAKE YOUR OWN BIOMES

06 Later in the game you'll want to start creating farms to generate items and summon bosses. The best way to do this is by creating biomes. Place a set number of blocks of a certain kind together and they'll convert the surrounding area to their type.

ARMOR UP
Forge a suit of armor from one material to get a defensive bonus.

STAY ORGANIZED
Make sure to name your chests to keep things in order.

BE PREPARED
Double-check that you're ready before taking on a boss.

TERRARIA

HARDMODE WORLD MAP

Bosses reborn
Defeated bosses make a comeback in Hardmode. Head to the Dungeon to fight the deadlier Skeletron Prime.

Corruption spreading
The Corruption expands rapidly and can overrun biomes in Hardmode if left unchecked.

The Hallow
The Hallow may look inviting with its unicorns and rainbows, but it's a formidable place.

Brave new world
Upon defeating the Wall of Flesh you'll find your world changed. Welcome to Hardmode.

"IN-GAME TIME IS IMPORTANT IN TERRARIA. IT IMPACTS ENEMIES THAT SPAWN"

3 BOSSES TO TRACK DOWN AND SLAY

1 EYE OF CTHULU
Likely the first boss you'll face, the Eye of Cthulu has a 33% chance of appearing at night once certain criteria are fulfilled.

Eye of Cthulhu

2 PLANTERA
You'll find Plantera in the underground Jungle biome in Hardmode. Clear a large area before summoning it to dodge its poisonous projectiles.

3 OCRAM
A Hardmode boss exclusive to the mobile and console versions of *Terraria*, Ocram spawns a ton of minions while peppering you with lasers and scythes.

BUILD YOUR FIRST HOUSE
CREATE A SECURE TERRARIA DWELLING

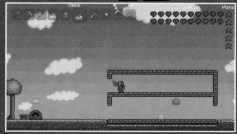

1 LAY THE GROUNDWORK
Clear out a suitable space. Find a spot near your spawn point and get to work clearing trees and earth to lay your floor.

2 ASSEMBLE A FRAME
Use stone or wood to put down a floor and draw walls and ceilings. Leave space for doors; you'll need to get in and out.

3 BUILD THE BASICS
Basic furniture includes doors and tables, fireplaces and torches, and a bed, which will act as your new spawn point.

4 SECURE THE PERIMETER
Adding background walls is vital. They make your house suitable for habitation and prevent zombies spawning inside!

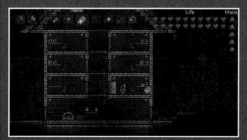

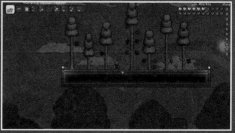

5 DECORATE AWAY
While you're waiting for roommates, personalize your house. Add books, vases, and windows if you have access to glass.

6 MEET THE NEIGHBORS
Your NPC roommates each have their own perks, ranging from special abilities to items for sale.

THE SIMS

LIFE IS WHAT YOU MAKE OF IT

Where would we be without *The Sims*? Not only is it one of the most successful gaming franchises on the planet, but it's also done a pretty fantastic job of establishing the life-simulation and world-building genres that we love so much today. There's something wonderful, isn't there, about guiding your young, hopeful Sim up from an infant to adult; guiding them through life and love,

into careers and new friendships, before inevitably bringing it all to an end by encouraging them to take a dip in a swimming pool and removing the ladder ... oops. But that's the glory of *The Sims*—it gives you all of the power and lets you choose what you want to do with it. There's never quite been another franchise like *The Sims*; may it keep us entertained forever.

TIME LINE

THE SIMS 2000
After nine years, *The Sims* is finally released, shipping over 16 million copies!

THE SIMS 2 2004
The Sims 2 expanded the gameplay, adding a 3-D game world.

TOP 5 CAREERS

1 PHOTOGRAPHER

Train your Sim as a photographer to capture moments of magic. Your house or studio will soon be full of your gorgeous pics!

2 ASTRONAUT

You can send your little Sim buddies out to explore the stars and planets so you can stay safely indoors.

3 ENTERTAINER

Make your dreams come true in *The Sims 4* by following the entertainer career path. The game will give you and your Sim the option to become either a comedian or a musician.

4 SCIENTIST

Because most Sims are super-smart, why not take your minions down the path of bettering humanity as a scientist?

5 SELF-EMPLOYED

You don't *have* to follow an official path. Go your own way and delight the neighborhood with your creations.

SIMS 3 2009
The Sims 3 was the largest release in PC gaming history.

SIMS 4 2014
Undoubtedly the finest version of the franchise to date.

EXCITE-O-METER

There's so much to do it'll last you for weeks:

+ Endless gameplay
+ Regular updates
− The extra packs cost real money

BEHIND THE SCENES
THE SIMS 4

6 DEVELOPMENT TRUE FACTS

NEW TEAM, NEW OPTIONS

01 The fourth edition of the popular life-simulation game was a collaboration between The Sims Studio and original developer Maxis, though legendary creator and mastermind Will Wright was not involved with its creation.

FEATURE CONTROVERSY

02 While *The Sims 4* did a lot to expand the classic gameplay, it also caused controversy as Maxis removed a handful of staple features from its latest release. Luckily, these were added later as DLC.

Meet the team at Maxis! These are the ladies and gentlemen who put together the game we just can't stop playing!

TALKING SIMLISH

04 You know Simlish, the nonsensical, fictional language found in *The Sims*? Carly Rae Jepsen actually rerecorded her 2015 megahit "Run Away With Me" in Simlish!

A MASSIVE UNDERTAKING

05 Every part of *The Sims 4* massively expands upon everything that's come before it— even parts you may take for granted. Take the sound design, for example. The team created half a million sound files to make the world feel more alive than any *Sims* game before.

GET CREATIVE

03 *The Sims 4* featured more creative tools, with the team recognizing how much players loved to tinker with every aspect of their Sims' lives. Create a Sim and Build Mode were made better than ever.

PIRATE PUNISHMENT

06 In an effort to battle piracy, Maxis integrated a mode into *The Sims 4* that would detect if you had an illegal copy of the game and then turn the graphics into a blurry, pixelated mess.

STATS

14 different classes to choose from

250 the highest level you can reach in a profession

You can join up to **5** different clubs at one time

133 different enemies across all biomes

TROVE

MINECRAFT MEETS WORLD OF WARCRAFT

Trove is quite a lot more than those two games named above. However, spend just five minutes in its blocky, MMO-styled world and you can't help think of Mojang's epic builder and Blizzard's MMO grandaddy.

While it does smack of those memorable greats, *Trove* has plenty of things to offer that are all its own. From its almost seamless open worlds that link together to create one huge, multi-themed hub, to the deep level of customization that enables you to change everything from your weapons to your hat, *Trove* has lots to offer.

This is an MMO (Massively Multiplayer Online—in other words, lots of people playing online together in the same game), so you can tackle all these tasks and quests alone or with friends.

TIPS & TRICKS

LEARN THE EQUIPS
You have four slots known as Equips that improve your character.

ALLIES ARE KEY!
The Ally slot gives you a friend to follow you and boost your stats.

TOP 5 CLASSES

KNIGHT

1 The jack of all trades, and an ideal choice for players new to *Trove*, the Knight is a melee character. His special Ability, Ultimate, restores health.

BOOMERANGER

2 The Boomeranger is one of a few characters that's both melee and ranged (they use swords and bows), meaning he's good for players that like to mix it up.

TOMB RAISER

3 With a trusty staff at his side, this magic-wielding dude can raise an army of minions to fight for you while damaging enemies with a piercing beam.

PIRATE CAPTAIN

4 Pirate Captain has a huge Plunderbuss, can trick enemies with his Pretend Pirate or blow them away with a Man-O-War. Definitely one for the sea dogs among you!

CHLOROMANCER

5 With a powerful staff and extra-useful wings, the Chloromancer is the perfect addition to your party. Her healing ability will help your teammates.

EXCITE-O-METER

A hack-n-slash with a *Minecraft* feel? Awesome!

+ So much to explore
+ Huge open world
− Unlocking blocks takes a long time

RAISE YOUR MASTER LEVEL
Cubits are the rare currency of the game. Raise your Master level to find them more easily.

TOP 10
CHANNELS WE LOVE

IHASCUPQUAKE
NUMBER OF FANS
77,034 (Twitch) 4,539,451 (YouTube)

iHasCupquake hails from Los Angeles and in the real world is called Tiffany. She first found popularity through her *Minecraft* streams, where she would build all kinds of things. With such huge success under her belt, Cupquake started to focus on other titles, too.

Minecraft remains a constant fixture, especially at seasonal times of year. Want a Christmas themed *Minecraft* video? iHasCupquake is the lady to go to.

CLOAKEDYOSHI
NUMBER OF FANS
**63,745 (Twitch)
6,795 (YouTube)**
Love *Super Mario Maker* but find the harder levels a challenge? This is why

streamers like CloakedYoshi exist. Taking on jaw-droppingly difficult courses, you can see exactly what it takes to be an expert.

STAMPY
NUMBER OF FANS
**769 (Twitch),
7,320,078 (YouTube)**
Stampy makes at least one *Minecraft* video a day and streams a host of other world-building games to boot. In addition he plays *Super Mario Maker* for which he also offers up tips.

KURTJMAC
NUMBER OF FANS
**43,708 (Twitch),
375,203 (YouTube)**
Known for a run of *Minecraft* streams, Kurtjmac once decided to simply walk west for over three years.

THEDIAMONDMINECART
NUMBER OF FANS
**17,0961 (Twitch),
10,446,927 (YouTube)**
TheDiamondMinecart has streamed *Minecraft* for over four years. His ongoing story of adventures feels like you're watching a *Minecraft* TV show.

SETHBLING
NUMBER OF FANS
252,453 (Twitch)
1,939,340 (YouTube),
If you're into the weird and wonderful creations that can come out of *Minecraft*, SethBling is for you.

THINKNOODLES
NUMBER OF FANS
7,818 (Twitch), 1,298,495 (YouTube)
Focusing more on adventuring and multiplayer than building, Thinknoodles is always happy and excited to play *Minecraft*. He does Christmas-themed videos, too.

PAULSOARESJR
NUMBER OF FANS
4,920 (Twitch),
1,316,181 (YouTube)
Paulsoaresjr is a serious *Minecraft* Dad, meaning he often sits down to play with his kids.

HI5TOSAFETY
NUMBER OF FANS **7,552 (Twitch)**
Hi5ToSafety suffers through *Super Mario Maker* so you don't have to! Taking on the hardest levels until he completes them, expect a lot of restarting and a lot of frustration as he refuses to quit.

"KNOW ANYTHING AND EVERYTHING ABOUT MINECRAFT"

LITTLE LIZARD GAMING
NUMBER OF FANS
25,955 (Twitch), 2,479,894 (YouTube)
Mods, tutorials, how to's, and exploring new content? That's Little Lizard Gaming in a nutshell, a stream dedicated to ensuring you know anything and everything about *Minecraft*. Don't forget the fun mash-ups!

000004

STATS

Over **6 million** levels created

68 sample courses included

Over **3.3 million** copies sold worldwide

4 different game styles for you to choose from

SUPER MARIO MAKER

MARIOS IN THE MILLIONS

You've probably played a *Mario* game or ten in your time, but have you ever considered making your own? The portly plumber's adventures have provided decades of fun to gamers of all ages, but behind the simple visuals of the classic 2-D *Mario* games lies a deceptively inventive and powerful set of tools.

With *Super Mario Maker*, Nintendo decided to open up that toolbox and share it with everyone. By making use of the Wii U gamepad, players can tap, drag, and draw their own levels to life before sharing them with the world. Not only does the game offer you the chance to step into the shoes of Shigeru Miyamoto and test your game-design mettle, but thanks to the community of millions you'll never run out of *Mario* levels again!

TIPS & TRICKS

HAVE A PLAN
Don't just throw stuff together; think ahead and you'll build better levels.

MIX IT UP
Variety is the spice of life. Try not to repeat yourself too much to keep it interesting.

TOP 5 COURSE ELEMENTS

GOOMBAS

1 *Super Mario Maker* lets you mutate classic enemies. Add wings to make them fly, draw them hard routes, or make them huge.

THWOMPS

2 The blocks of stone are deadly to touch and can quickly crush Mario, so try arranging a corridor of them to really force players into a speedy run.

SUPER STARS

3 A Super Star can change the feel of a level. Put one in a dangerous location and you create a risk/reward scenario that creates a tough decision for players.

MYSTERY MUSHROOMS

5 This item works with an amiibo of your choice to change Mario into an 8-bit version of another character, from Pikachu to Pac-Man.

KOOPA CLOWN CARS

4 You'll mostly use these to transport Mario, but they can also carry enemies, like Piranha Plants and Chain Chomps, and will scale in size to fit them in.

DON'T OVERCOMPLICATE
Try not to clutter up your level with too much. Simplicity is often the key to a good course.

EXCITE-O-METER
Making our own *Mario* levels is a dream come true
+ Hundreds of items
+ Share your levels!
− No checkpoints

TOP 10

SUPER MARIO MAKER LEVELS

WARIO WARE INC
Creator: Steve

Wario Ware Inc from British user Steve is one of the more frustrating courses, but it's so much fun to play. Inspired by the *Wario Ware* series, this level is essentially a series of mini-games that task you with overcoming different obstacles. None of them are particularly difficult and each one last seconds at the most, but it's the sheer sense of variety (one minute you're outrunning a green shell you set off, the next you're leaping over spike pits) that sets it apart.

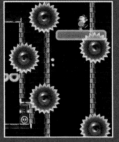

SUPER MEAT BROS
Creator: GameXplain
Super Meat Bros is all about speed and perfect timing. It's full of buzzsaws and chain chomps just waiting to get you.

- - - - - - - - - - - - - - - -

MARIO GEAR SOLID
Creator: Nick
This level relies on the use of bombs and expert timing to create a rewarding and memorable slice of *Mario Maker* fun.

TRESPASS IN THE MANNER U PLEASE
Creator: David Hellman
Trespass in the Manner U Please is an airship level that's got a Metroidvania feel (a popular type of open platformer). You don't need to rush through it, and there are lots of different routes to take.

SUPER SHMUP BROS
Creator: Andre GX
Rather than going for the usual platformer, Andre GX instead gives us a shoot-'em-up. Start in Bowser's flying car before letting loose with those fireballs.

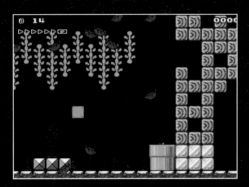

GREEN HILL ZONE

Creator: TRSF Lucas

This sends two gaming greats crashing into one another as Sonic speeds around a great course.

CASTLEVANIA

Creator: IGA

Okay, this one is really special. Rather than being a straight-up fan love letter to the old *Castlevania* games, this course was designed by the man who helped create them in the first place, Koji Igarashi.

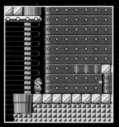

HAIL-FIRE PEAKS

Creator: Glu

This is all about the best of *Mario*. There are great platform challenges and lots of dangers to dodge.

"YOU'LL FIND YOURSELF LEAPING OVER MONSTER-RIDDEN PITS"

RAIDERS OF THE LOST COIN

Creator: Nick

In true *Indiana Jones* style, you'll find yourself leaping over monster-ridden pits and even outrunning a giant cannonball as you try to knock out all the Goombas in front of you with your fireballs.

THE DOC MAKES A HOUSE CALL

Creator: Kyle

Taking the phrase "Bowser's Inside Story" to a new level, this sends Dr. Mario inside his biggest enemy, where he has to leap through challenging platforms. You'll get plenty of coins and applause for it.

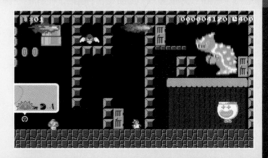

TIPS & TRICKS

SUPER MARIO MAKER

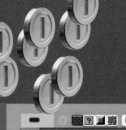

8 ESSENTIAL TIPS

KEEP LEVELS SHORT

01 Unlike *LittleBigPlanet* you can't create checkpoints, so make sure your creation doesn't take too long to finish. Some of the very best *Mario* levels use a short amount of space to show off the best ideas.

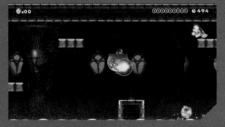

USE THE UNDO DOG

02 Making mistakes is an important part of making a great level. The Eraser is great for removing unwanted bits from your level, while the Undo Dog is ideal for getting rid of recent errors.

CLICK TO CHANGE HAND

03 If you press down on the thumbstick on your gamepad you'll be able to change it from a right hand to a left, change the color of its skin, and even turn it into a paw!

QUICK TRICKS

GET NEW CHARACTERS
Complete the 100 Mario Challenge or buy amiibo figures to unlock characters.

A PERFECT TEN
You can only upload ten levels until your creations are rated.

GET INSPIRED

04 *Super Mario Maker* doesn't have a proper story, but try the 100 Mario Challenge to get inspired. Everything you see in these levels can be remade by you, so get playing and get some ideas.

DON'T FORGET TO GO UP

05 Just because you're making a *Mario* level doesn't mean you have to make it in a traditional side-scrolling way. Vines are perfect for going vertical and moving from one platform to another.

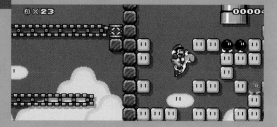

CHOOSE YOUR TEMPLATE

06 You can use elements from all major *Mario* games in *Super Mario Maker*. Each game has slightly different power-ups, so play around.

PUBLISH YOUR LEVELS

07 A big part of the fun is sharing your level with other gamers. Not only does this mean you can try out other people's creations for ideas, but rate them, too. So make sure you really get those creative juices flowing.

GET PLANNING!

08 Once you've played around a little, grab a pencil and paper and plan your level. Being able to see your entire level will help you figure out where to place platforms, power-ups, and more.

USE THOSE DOORS
Doors can transport you to another location, but you can only use four per course.

COPY AND PASTE
Use your gamepad to copy sections of your level and use them elsewhere to save time.

LEGO WORLDS

MOVE OVER, MINECRAFT?

Minecraft has enjoyed world domination for *years* now—for a game that started out on an obscure forum in the middle of nowhere (well, the Internet's version of nowhere), the crafty block game has done *awfully* well for itself. Well, a new challenger is here to take the crown off *Minecraft's* head. And its name is LEGO.

TTGames has been making LEGO games for a *long* time now—over ten years, in fact. As a result, it knows how to make that fun, constructive LEGO feel work well in a game. What better way is there to show that off than in a world-building, block-bashing exploration game? LEGO inspired the original *Minecraft* in the first place, so now everything has come full circle and gamers can safely return to the masters of the building block.

TIME LINE

GOING UNDERGROUND
JUNE 1, 2015
The first game update lets players explore caves.

UNDER THE SEA
AUGUST 10, 2015
New creatures, figures, and water!

TOP 5 LEGO WORLDS FACTS

1 MAKE ANYTHING

Want to make a cowboy's ranch? Go ahead. What about an elven village with riverside trees? Fine. How about something scarier? Mountains, fire, and dragons? That's cool, too. Seriously, you can do *anything* you want.

2 YOU'LL BE SAFE ONLINE

LEGO Worlds will only let you play with people you invite, so if any random people start trying to join, you can decline them entry. Always have fun, but remember … always play safe.

3 IGNORE THE BUILDING!

The game caters to players that just want to explore a world, and has a huge selection of already playable levels. They might even inspire you to make your own.

4 CONSTANT UPDATES

LEGO Worlds keeps adding playable things into its system, meaning that over time, there are simply more and more things to do.

5 NOT HOLDING YOU BACK

This game reminds you it's about creation. Go underground to examine caves, or float up to the clouds for their block-yet-fluffy shapes.

QUEST WISHES
OCTOBER 30, 2015
Missions are added, and bugs are fixed.

GETTING THERE!
DECEMBER 12, 2015
New quests, creatures, and characters!

EXCITE-O-METER

The most exciting LEGO game for years!

+ Massive open world
+ Cool stuff to build
− Only in alpha, so it's not finished yet

STATS

It costs over **$600** to buy all *LEGO Dimensions* characters

LEGO Star Wars has sold over **30 million copies**

LEGO games are **19** years old!

Over **40 billion** LEGO figures have been sold!

COOLEST LEGO GAMES

BLOCKING ALL OVER THE WORLD

It may not have started as one of gaming's biggest franchises—*Mario, Sonic, Pokémon,* and *Mega Man* had that advantage—but LEGO has certainly caught up fast. The blocky little characters, the creativity it brings out in players, and that addictive collect 'em all gameplay made sure that you just couldn't put any of the 64 currently released LEGO games down.

Yes, 64 is a lot—and they've only been released since 1997, which means the developers had to produce three games a year! To save you from going back to play them all (because, honestly, they're not all as good as *LEGO Jurassic World*), we've taken the liberty of letting you in on a little secret—the four coolest LEGO games that have ever been made.

TIME LINE

LEGO GOES DIGITAL 1997
LEGO Island is released, and we finally get to play with LEGO on a computer.

THE FORCE 2005
The first *LEGO Star Wars* game is released.

TOP 4 COOLEST LEGO GAMES

LEGO ISLAND

1 The oldest LEGO game was made almost 20 years ago in 1997. It's like an early *Minecraft* game; there's no real story, and you're free to explore a colorful island at your leisure. It hasn't aged *that* well, but without it, we wouldn't have the LEGO games we do today.

LEGO STAR WARS: THE COMPLETE SAGA

2 Did you know that this is one of the best-selling games *ever*? You can play it on almost anything—from phones to old consoles. It's *Star Wars: Episodes I–VII*, with that humor the LEGO games achieve so well.

LEGO MARVEL SUPER HEROES

3 Like *The Avengers*, but better, this game features all of your favorite heroes: Spider-Man, the Fantastic Four, the X-Men, and more. The coolest bit? Saving Marvel mastermind Stan Lee from peril in every level.

LEGO DIMENSIONS

4 You're playing as Batman, but Scooby-Doo and his pals are in a fix, so you call on Homer Simpson for help. In *LEGO Dimensions*, this can be a reality. This game is basically a box full of all the LEGO bricks in the world, inside your controller.

LOSING TOUCH 2010
LEGO tries (and fails) to mimic *World of Warcraft's* success in MMORPGs.

BOUNCE BACK! 2015
LEGO Dimensions releases with dozens of franchises included.

EXCITE-O-METER

From *LEGO Star Wars* to *LEGO Dimensions*, there's sure to be something for you in this franchise

➕ The biggest names

➕ Great level design!

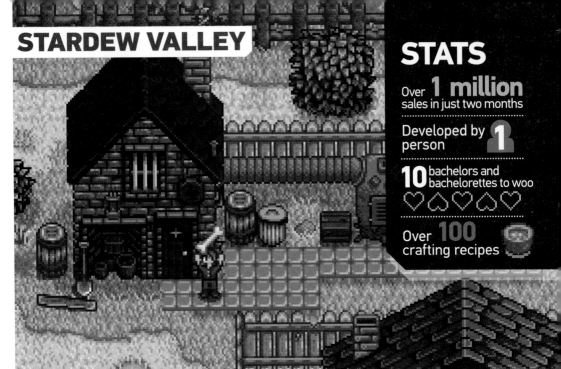

STATS

Over **1 million** sales in just two months

Developed by 1 person

10 bachelors and bachelorettes to woo

♡ △ ♡ △ ♡

Over **100** crafting recipes

STARDEW VALLEY

RELEASE YOUR INNER FARMER

How long have we spent searching for the new *Harvest Moon*? It's been a few years, at least. But that's okay, because *Stardew Valley* is here now, and it's the spiritual sequel to *Harvest Moon* that we always wanted.

Gorgeous pixel art, hours of original music, and gameplay that you won't be able to put down—this is a game that will consume your life ... and you might pick up a few agricultural tips along the way, as you grow and maintain the farm you inherited from your grandfather. Don't let its style fool you, *Stardew Valley* is an incredibly deep game—just don't forget to water the crops before you go to bed each night, otherwise you'll wake up to a farmland fiasco in the morning.

TIPS & TRICKS

SLEEP IS IMPORTANT
If you stay out past 2 A.M. you'll collapse. Be home by midnight!

TV EVERY MORNING
The weather reports on the TV will be integral as your farm grows.

TOP 4 CROPS TO GROW EACH SEASON

SPRING: YEAR ONE

1 Starting out, you'll want to get cauliflower in the ground immediately. At just 105 gold per plant, it'll generate a ton of cash in the seasonal period. You can buy them at Pierre's General Store. Remember to check the bulletin board there.

SUMMERTIME

2 When it comes to enjoying the summer, there's only one fruit you need concern yourself with: blueberries. Raw blueberries yield 880 gold profit per crop, or you can make jelly and sell it for 210 gold.

AUTUMN: YEAR ONE

3 Another season, another berry. You'll want to start stocking preservers around now since it'll become harder in winter. Cranberries don't make as much money, but they can be stored in the fridge for later!

WINTER BLUES

4 Wintertime is not very fun for farmers. Take this time to tend to your crops and take stock of your resources. If you want to plant something get a Fruit Tree—although it'll take 28 days to grow.

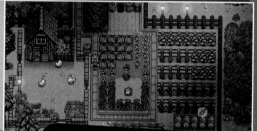

DIG IT UP

If you come across worms, pull out your hoe and start digging to unearth special items.

EXCITE-O-METER

Who knew farming could be so relaxing and fun?

+ Loads to see and do
+ Constantly updated
+ A beautiful world

STARDEW VALLEY

DEVELOPER PROFILE

NAME Eric Barone
AGE 26
FAVORITE GAMES
Harvest Moon,
Secret Of Mana

From part-time theatre actor to millionaire game creator in just two weeks, Eric "ConcernedApe" Barone single-handedly developed *Stardew Valley* over the last four years in an attempt to create a better version of the ever-popular *Harvest Moon* games. As one of the most successful indie games of 2016, *Stardew Valley* has been a labor of love for Barone; working up to 70 hours a week on the game in his spare time. But it just goes to show that with a great idea and a little perseverance, anything is possible.

STATS

It took
4 years
to develop
Stardew Valley

88 Metascore
on Metacritic

17
animals
in the game

10 hours
of original music
recorded by Barone

**41 characters
to meet**

Despite having very little knowledge of game design, Eric Barone set about on a four-year journey to create *Stardew Valley*.

It started as a *Harvest Moon* clone though it quickly evolved into something much bigger.

STARDEW'S INSPIRATION

RUNE FACTORY

An RPG that has close ties with *Harvest Moon*, *Rune Factory* takes players to a town to fight in dungeons and foster new friendships.

HARVEST MOON

Stardew Valley is essentially a successor to *Harvest Moon*. You take control of a beaten-up farm and restore it to glory ... sound familiar?

MINECRAFT

Barone looked to the success of *Minecraft* creator for inspiration; he's living proof that hard work and dedication can pay off.

GAMER CHALLENGE

CHECK YOUR GAMING CRED

01 How many animals are there in *Stardew Valley*?

02 Which character can heal in *Trove*?

03 How do you get hold of a Super Mushroom in *Super Mario Maker*?

04 Which world-building game series debuted in 2000?

05 Which blocky game has sold over 70 million copies?

06 How many playable characters are included in *LEGO Worlds*?

07 In which game can you play as Bart Simpson, Batman, and Scooby-Doo?

08 Which creation game features a mystical tree god?

09 What is the name of the made-up language spoken by people in *The Sims*?

10 What animal helps you undo mistakes when building levels in *Super Mario Maker*?

11 Which game, to be released in 2017, will feature a journalist called Jade?

12 What is the name of the developer behind *The Sims 4*?

13 What's the real name of "the Minecraft Dad"?

14 How many game styles are there to choose from in *Super Mario Maker*?

15 What year was the first *LEGO* game released?

16 How many people made *Stardew Valley*?

HOW DID YOU SCORE?

0–5 **Gaming Noob**—you need to step it up!

6–10 **Casual Gamer**—you could do better!

11–15 **Hardcore Gamer**—you know your stuff!

16 **Gaming God**—great job, you totally rock!

ANSWERS 01. SEVENTEEN 02. CHLOROMANCER 03. PLACE AN AMIIBO ON THE GAME PAD 04. THE SIMS 05. MINECRAFT 06. FORTY 07. LEGO DIMENSIONS 08. KWAAN 09. SIMLISH 10. UNDO DOG 11. BEYOND GOOD & EVIL 2 12. MAXIS 13. PAUL SOARES JR. 14. FOUR 15. 1997 16. ONE

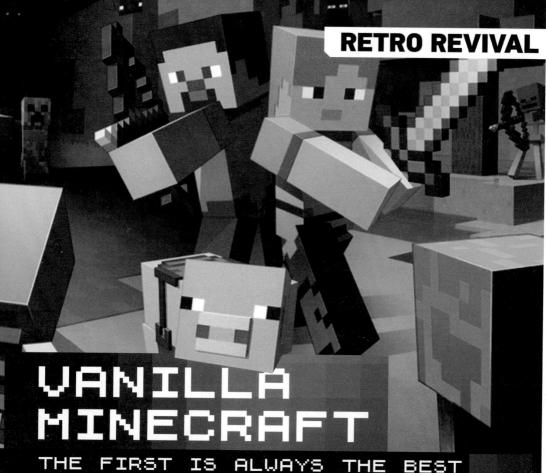

VANILLA MINECRAFT

THE FIRST IS ALWAYS THE BEST

FIRST RELEASED
November, 18, 2011

COPIES SOLD
Over 70 million

DEVELOPER
Mojang

"Vanilla" *Minecraft* **isn't a tasty treat, despite how it sounds. Instead, it refers to the original, unmodified version you probably already have on your computer.**

Amazingly, though, there are certain modifications that can be added without losing its "vanilla" status. But if you want to enjoy Survival Mode within a vanilla setting, you need to go back to basics.

Vanilla *Minecraft* shines because it retains the simplicity that made the original so good. It's a perfect way for beginners to learn the ropes; soon you may be tempted to make the jump and start modding to your heart's content. Just remember where the love started ...

STATS

You can play *Minecraft Story Mode* on 10 different devices!

Choose from 6 character designs for Jesse

There are over 22 characters to meet!

There will be 8 episodes

MINECRAFT STORY MODE

EVERYONE ENJOYS A GOOD BLOCK PARTY

Minecraft is so much fun that we spend hours making amazing structures, but the one thing it's always been lacking is a proper story. That's why it's so nice to play this new plot-driven adventure game, featuring Jesse, a passionate *Minecraft* newbie who sets out to find the five heroes who saved the world.

You might find the characters familiar if you're a regular *Minecraft*-er. Each of the friends you make in the game were based on real-life types of *Minecraft* player. You've got the combat-mad folks, the crazy constructors, the explorers, the geniuses, and the thieves (as well as many more, besides). The episode-by-episode way that *Story Mode* plays out is great for making you take in the story a bit at a time—perfect if you've only got a short time to play games each night.

TIPS & TRICKS

REPLAY AND RETRY
Play a few times choosing different options to see all the endings!

CREEPER FIGHT!
Don't be afraid of Creepers—just take them out one at a time.

TOP 5 MINECRAFT CHARACTERS

JESSE

1 A kind-hearted and passionate *Minecraft* newcomer, Jesse is the hero that you will shape through your choices.

GABRIEL

2 Considered the greatest warrior ever, Gabriel is a true diamond in the rough. He's strong, brave, and determined to help people.

ELLEGAARD

3 A smart inventor who can't stop the constant flow of ideas coming out of her head, Ellegaard is smug and a little arrogant. She loves eating bread, and has a bad habit of shooting down people she doesn't think are as intelligent as she is.

MAGNUS

4 Magnus is fun—he's a demolition expert. Despite his shifty appearance, he's one of the most noble allies. He loves blowing things up, but only if it helps people.

SOREN

5 The "mad professor" character, Soren is willing to endanger his life in the name of science. He discovered the Command Block, and is an eccentric, loyal friend.

UPGRADE IT ALL

You can craft in this, so upgrading your items is a great idea.

EXCITE-O-METER

Minecraft gets an awesome story for the first time!

+ We love *Minecraft*!
+ Brilliantly written
+ More episodes still to come!

BESIEGE

STATS

735,000 views
on Spiderling Studios'
YouTube channel

6 islands of levels
and puzzles to solve

56 different types of
blocks to build with

11 types of engines that
can be created using
the blocks available

BESIEGE
BUILD YOUR OWN WAR MACHINE!

You've played *Angry Birds*, right? Well, believe it or not, *Besiege* is a lot like that. It's a physics-based puzzle game, but rather than flinging grumpy parrots through the air, you're building your own deadly machines as you try to defeat the enemy, destroy the castle, or attack important structures. But what is most impressive about this game is that it's actually more of a sandbox experience, where you can use your own creativity to find solutions to the different challenges you'll come up against. You're given the tools, but there is no "correct" way to succeed, and so your creations will look completely different from those of your friends. *Besiege* can be pretty challenging, but because it's so inventive you'll have fun just trying to construct the greatest medieval war machines.

TIPS & TRICKS

BE SAFE
Include wooden panels on weak points of your machine to stop archery damage.

STRENGTH WINS
Remember to create sturdy machines. Don't let good plans fall apart.

TOP 4 CREATIONS

ROTATING TANK

1 Cannons play a big part in *Besiege*, but this creative player managed to build his very own tank. Best of all is the turret. It fires six cannons at once and can be rotated to take aim at whatever you want to destroy.

WASP

2 Code-named the WASP, this creation is a very quick, easy way to control a race car. It's extremely sturdy, and it can be forced to stand upright and still be driven around. It's not a deadly machine, but it's a great build.

DRAGON

3 The moving parts are technically impressive, but the fact that you can use a fire-breathing dragon with spikes for claws to defeat the enemy is what stands out the most.

GYROCOPTER

4 Who said your creations had to stay on the ground? It must've taken some time to build this flying device. Imagine how satisfying it would be to use it to wipe out crowds below.

BOMBS AWAY!
Explosives are great, but if you don't build a catapult properly it could cause more damage to you!

EXCITE-O-METER

Besiege offers total creative freedom. It's awesome!

+ Constantly updates
+ Super replayable
− Short campaign

TOP 10
AWESOME WORLD-BUILDING GAMES

KERBAL SPACE PROGRAM

Think building a spaceship is a simple case of slapping rockets on the side of a tin can? Sadly not, and *Kerbal Space Program* shows just how difficult flying off into space really is! Creating different rockets to see what happens is ridiculously good fun, especially if you can power your creations into space.

FORTRESSCRAFT EVOLVED!

This *Minecraft*-like game involves creating factories with extractors, which power your base to fend off aliens. Grow it enough and you might even get to explore other planets.

DON'T STARVE

The aim of *Don't Starve* is ... well, not to go hungry. You have to build campfires, then defences for your base, and the rest is up to you. It's difficult but the way you put your world together is strangely compelling.

MANYLAND

Designed as an online sandbox, *Manyland* lets players create anything they want and share it. You can build mini-games, play music, and learn about programming.

KWAAN

With no combat, no killing and no competition, *Kwaan* is one of the most relaxing games ever. The community has to work together to build a world, tend to the ecosystem, and care for the god tree Kwaan. There are even spaces for doodling to satisfy your creative itch.

AWESOME WORLD-BUILDING GAMES

GNOMORIA

This village-building game has some serious depth. *Gnomoria* might not be pretty, but there's so much to do, you could be playing it forever.

SIMPLEPLANES

Think you can build a plane? *SimplePlanes* shows there is much more skill involved. Not only is your creativity challenged, but so is your brain and your smarts.

FOLK TALE

For those of you who love RPGs, *Folk Tale* is the perfect choice! From village building to adventuring, there is plenty to get stuck into here.

> "GNOMORIA MIGHT NOT BE PRETTY, BUT THERE'S SO MUCH TO DO, YOU COULD BE PLAYING IT FOREVER"

UNTURNED

If you enjoy fighting zombies in *Minecraft*, then try *Unturned*. You will scavenge for supplies, cooperate with other players, and build forts in this zombie survival game. The emphasis is on fighting and not creating, but you'll need both to survive.

UNIVERSE SANDBOX 2

You've built towns. You've built worlds. Can you build a universe? This ridiculously in-depth game lets you control gravity, climate, and more as you put planets together. It's beautiful, breathtaking, and brilliant.

WHICH WORLD BUILDING GAME IS RIGHT FOR YOU?

ARE YOU A FAN OF OPEN SANDBOX-STYLE GAMES?

YES

DO YOU LIKE EXPLORING TO COLLECT RESOURCES THAT YOU CAN USE TO MAKE TOOLS AND BUILDINGS?

NO

DO YOU LIKE BUILDING THINGS THAT NEED TO BE CAREFULLY PLANNED OUT?

YES

DO YOU PREFER A FANTASY SETTING OVER REALISM?

NO

YES

NO

ARE YOU INTERESTED IN GOING BEHIND THE SCENES OF GAME MAKING?

NO

NO

WOULD YOU PREFER A GAME WITH ENEMIES TO FIGHT (OR RUN FROM), HAZARDS TO AVOID, AND OTHER DANGERS?

YES

NO

YES

DO YOU WANT MAKING FRIENDS WITH CHARACTERS TO BE KEY TO THE GAME?

YES

NO

DO YOU LIKE GAMES WITH LOTS TO LEARN?

YES

NO

DO YOU WANT TO MAKE YOUR OWN GAMES ONE DAY?

YES

NO

IS BEING ABLE TO EASILY PLAY WITH FRIENDS IMPORTANT TO YOU?

NO

YES

THE SIMS 4
The Sims 4 places a bigger focus on personalities and interacting with other characters.

STARDEW VALLEY
This farming sim requires careful planning to manage your plot of land well.

MARIO MAKER
A game that lets you make, play, and share your own *Mario* levels is a must.

LEGO WORLDS
LEGO Worlds isn't finished yet! That means you can play as the game develops.

TERRARIA
With its focus on exploration, crafting, and building, *Terraria* is described as a 2-D *Minecraft*.

MINECRAFT
Brilliant gameplay, unique monsters, and playing with friends means *Minecraft* is one of the best!

MOST AWESOME

WORLD-BUILDING
ACHIEVEMENTS & TROPHIES!

TIME TO TAKE ON THE WORLD!

Some games give you achievements just for playing. Others hand them out when you finish a level. However, world-building games are a bit tougher. With so much to do and so many places to explore in games like *Minecraft*, *Terraria,* and *Sim City*, knowing what the trophies are, let alone earning them, can be a big challenge.

That's where our handy guide comes in. On top of helping you to set up a happy family in *The Sims*, or a perfect metropolis in *Cities: Skylines*, this is how to snag all the pesky achievements and trophies that are easy to miss while you're out having world-building fun.

Let's get to it!

ACHIEVEMENTS & TROPHIES!

MINECRAFT

Trophy On A Rail
Travel by mine cart to a point at least 1,640ft away from where you started

COOLEST ACHIEVEMENT

SCREAMRIDE

Achievement Don't. Look. Down.

Build a roller coaster with a drop height of 624 feet

You can only use a limited amount of track, so keep an eye on how you're spending it. Instead of making long and winding roller coasters, think quick and compact. Spend a few yards on a straight track to let cars build up speed, send them into a big dip, then take them up.

UNCOVER THE MAP
01 Explore the map, as far in every direction as you can, until you find a nice big area of flat land, like ice.

GET THE ORE
02 Get down the mines and grab Iron Ore. You'll need 198 Iron Ingots for the track, and five for the cart.

MOST ANNOYING ACHIEVEMENT

THE SIMS 4

Achievement Over Achiever

Have a Sim complete five Aspirations

Pick the five Aspirations that take the least effort! More specifically, pick five that your Sim can do on their own: If you're relying on making friends, you're making things harder for yourself. Sims can achieve Bodybuilding, Computer Whiz, Musical Genius, Bestselling Author, and Paint Extraordinaire by themselves.

LAY IT OUT
03 You may need to lay out powered rails every now and then to keep up your speed. Now off you go!

ACHIEVEMENTS & TROPHIES!

CITIES: SKYLINES

 Achievement Pioneer
Create your first city

Starting your city off is simple enough, but it's worth remembering a few vital pointers. Create a highway that goes straight down the middle. Keep industrial areas away from houses, but spread services like police stations and public transport evenly around, so everywhere in your city is covered.

MINECRAFT

Trophy When Pigs Fly
Fly a pig off a cliff

Put a saddle on a pig, get a carrot on a fishing rod, and off you go! Getting this achievement isn't enough—do it in style! Jump through a ring of fire, or jump into battle riding your trusty pig steed.

SIM CITY

Achievement UK Character
Have 10,000 Sims get picked up by a double-decker bus from the double-decker terminal

Once you've built a double-decker terminal this achievement pretty much works itself out, that is as long as you can keep your city running. What's weird is the name. Of all the things the British are famous for, who knows how the makers of *Sim City* settled on double-decker buses. How about fish and chips? Soccer? The Queen?! Or why not make the achievement about making a cup of tea?

ACHIEVEMENTS & TROPHIES!

TERRARIA

🏆 **Trophy** To Hell and Back
You have gone to the Underworld and back without dying

Get the best equipment you can (try the Necro armor, the Muramasa, and a decent bow with flaming arrows) and stay on your guard. To get it more easily, dig straight down to the Underworld and then climb by building wooden platforms. But that's cheating—try to do it for real!

EASIEST ACHIEVEMENTS

THE SIMS 4

Achievement Channel Surfer

Sims are lazy creatures, so this achievement—listening to all the different radio stations and watching all the TV channels—is easy peasy.

TERRARIA

Achievement Timber

To get this one, all you have to do is cut down a tree—to be honest, it'd be more of an achievement if you could finish *Terraria without* unlocking it.

SCREAMRIDE

Achievement I Hope You Have Insurance

It's easy, but this one is still fun. Build a roller coaster and then crash. We recommend putting down some sharp corners then holding accelerate.

END GAME

MINECRAFT: BATTLE MODE

Create a world and fight alongside friends in the all-new Battle mode

What better way to end our World-Building extravaganza than with the biggest game in the world? *Minecraft* recently added a dedicated multiplayer mode that sees you facing off against other players with premade weapon sets and rules!